Machines at Work

Tugboats

by Cari Meister

Bullfrog Books

Ideas for Parents and Teachers

Bullfrog Books let children practice reading informational text at the earliest reading levels. Repetition, familiar words, and photo labels support early readers.

Before Reading

- Discuss the cover photo. What does it tell them?

- Look at the picture glossary together. Read and discuss the words.

Read the Book

- "Walk" through the book and look at the photos. Let the child ask questions. Point out the photo labels.

- Read the book to the child, or have him or her read independently.

After Reading

- Prompt the child to think more. Ask: Have you ever seen a tugboat? Was it at work? What was it pushing?

Bullfrog Books are published by Jump!
5357 Penn Avenue South
Minneapolis, MN 55419
www.jumplibrary.com

Library of Congress Cataloging-in-Publication Data

Names: Meister, Cari.
Title: Tugboats / by Cari Meister.
Description: Minneapolis, Minnesota: Jump!, Inc., [2017]
Series: Machines at work
Audience: Age 5–8. | Audience: K to grade 3.
Includes index.
Identifiers: LCCN 2016002948 (print)
LCCN 2016012037 (ebook)
ISBN 9781620313701 (hardcover: alk. paper)
ISBN 9781620314883 (paperback)
ISBN 9781624964176 (ebook)
Subjects: LCSH: Tugboats—Juvenile literature.
Classification: LCC VM464 .M45 2017 (print)
LCC VM464 (ebook) | DDC 623.82/32—dc23
LC record available at http://lccn.loc.gov/2016002948

Editor: Jenny Fretland VanVoorst
Series Designer: Ellen Huber
Book Designer: Leah Sanders
Photo Researcher: Olympia Shannon

Photo Credits: All photos by Shutterstock except: Alamy, 10–11, 18; Angela N Perryman/Shutterstock.com, 22; Getty, 4, 6–7; iStock, 19, 20–21; Sheila Fitzgerald/Shutterstock.com, 16–17; Thinkstock, 22br; 123RF, 8–9, 23tr.

Printed in the United States of America at Corporate Graphics in North Mankato, Minnesota.

Table of Contents

Tugboats at Work 4

Parts of a Tugboat 22

Picture Glossary 23

Index 24

To Learn More 24

Tugboats at Work

Toot! Toot!

A tugboat
is at work.

A tug is small.

But it is very strong.

It has a powerful engine.
It can move a boat
many times its size!

It has a big winch.
It hooks to a ship.
It will not break.

winch

Look at the
narrow canal.

How does a ship
get through?

A tug pulls it.

How does a tanker get back to sea?

Tugs push it.

15

How does a cargo ship dock?

A tug spins it.

Here comes a log raft.

Oh, no! It is stuck.

What can help?
A tugboat can!
Toot! Toot!

Parts of a Tugboat

hull
The main part of a tugboat that includes the sides, deck, and bottom. Tugboats have heavy hulls so that they can partially sink and are better able to push large ships.

winch
A machine with a rope or chain attached that is used for pulling.

propeller
An object with two or more blades that helps a ship move.

keel
A long piece of metal or wood that is on the bottom of the boat; it gives a tugboat strength.

Picture Glossary

canal
A long, narrow waterway.

engine
A machine that changes energy into mechanical motion.

cargo ship
A large ship that transports goods.

tanker
A ship that transports liquids.

Index

boat 9

canal 13

docking 17

engine 9

log raft 18

pulling 13

pushing 14

ship 10, 13, 17

spinning 17

strong 6

tanker 14

winch 10

To Learn More

Learning more is as easy as 1, 2, 3.

1) Go to www.factsurfer.com

2) Enter "tugboats" into the search box.

3) Click the "Surf" button to see a list of websites.

With factsurfer.com, finding more information is just a click away.